Queer Questions
Straight Talk

Queer Questions
Straight Talk

108 frank & provocative questions it's OK to ask
your lesbian, gay or bisexual loved one

ABBY DEES

st. lynn's press

PITTSBURGH

Queer Questions Straight Talk
108 Frank & Provocative Questions it's OK to Ask Your Lesbian,
Gay or Bi Loved One

Copyright © 2010 by Abby Dees

ISBN-13: 978-0-9819615-2-1

Library of Congress Control Number: 2010922333
CIP information available upon request

First Edition, 2010

St. Lynn's Press • POB 18680 • Pittsburgh, PA 15236
412.466.0790 • www.stlynnspress.com

Typesetting – Holly Wensel, Network Printing Services
Cover design – Heidi Spurgin
Editor – Catherine Dees

Printed in the United States of America
on recycled paper

This title and all of St. Lynn's Press books may be purchased for educational, business, or sales promotional use. For information please write:
Special Markets Department . St. Lynn's Press . POB 18680 . Pittsburgh, PA 15236

10 9 8 7 6 5 4 3 2 1

For Traci

Table of Contents

Introduction

"The time has come," the Walrus said,
"To talk of many things:
Of shoes – and ships – and sealing-wax –
Of cabbages – and kings –"
Lewis Carroll, from Through the Looking Glass

Welcome!

If you're reading this book it means one of two things: you want to have an honest and loving dialogue with someone in your life about what it means to be lesbian, gay or bi... or someone in your life wants to have an honest and loving dialogue with you. How wonderful for both of you.

You might be a straight child with a gay parent, a bi daughter with a straight parent, a lesbian friend or sister, a gay brother or buddy. Perhaps you have already had some heartfelt conversations with your loved one but there's still so much more to talk about. If you're straight, you might have concerns about your loved one's identity or choices; if you're lesbian, gay or bi, maybe *you* simply want your loved one to know that you're ready for whatever nutty questions they've got about your life (the last thing you want is for them to feel uncomfortable, or to worry that asking would be prying). If any of this sounds familiar, then *Queer Questions Straight Talk* was written with you in mind.

Housekeeping note: Instead of repeating "lesbian, gay or bi" umpteen times throughout the book, I'll be using the zippier shorthand term "LesBiGay."

Some background

I've been an "out" lesbian for 25 years (I've been a lesbian for...well, longer than that). I have been blessed with a ton of fabulous straight friends and allies, and my family (all straight to my knowledge, except maybe for one aunt) showed up in full festive regalia when I married my partner in 2008. In a time when so many non-straight people have to hide who they are for fear of being utterly rejected by the people they love, I couldn't be more fortunate.

Yet, questions about what it means to be a lesbian (in my case) still come up all the time. Just when I think everyone I know is on the same page, someone will sheepishly say something that makes me mutter quietly to myself, *You've gotta be kidding...You've waited ten years to ask me if there's a symbolic gay reason I'm handy with a socket wrench?* I'm actually glad they asked, but it makes me wonder what other things are going unsaid – important things.

There are millions of good and kind people who have a LesBiGay friend or loved one – but until they found out, never thought they knew a gay person who wasn't on TV with a candelabra. It's no surprise, then, that they'd have questions, concerns, and maybe more than a few misguided preconceptions. I'd hope they could feel free to talk about it without the fear of looking "politically incorrect" or, worse, homophobic.

It's too easy to label someone who is new to this whole thing as a homophobe, as if by virtue of having a LesBiGay son, daughter, mother or friend, they should automatically be totally hip to the lingo and the theoretical underpinnings of "queer culture." Given this, I'm inclined to forgive someone who chooses to stay quiet rather than risk saying something stupid or hurtful.

But silence keeps people apart. There's got to be a time and place to ask the real questions and ponder the answers – a time and place to learn a little more about your loved one. This book comes out of my very strong belief that if you are asking with love in your heart, there are no stupid questions.

Queer Questions Straight Talk is your permission slip to put an end to the awkward silence, with 108 questions that you might have (or maybe never have) considered before…

and some gentle guidance along the way. It is, very simply, about getting the conversation going, with love and patience and – yes, I know you can do it – an open mind. Both of you.

How to use this book

Each of the seven short chapters starts with an introduction to a particular aspect of LesBiGay life (Identity, Religion & Spirituality, Sex, etc.). I'll share with you some of my personal experiences and those of others – some whose names you might recognize – along with a few bits of wisdom for how to make the most of your conversation.

And all those questions? They come out of conversations I've had with straight and LesBiGay people, running the gamut from frequently-asked to no-one's-ever-asked-me-that-before. Some are based on old stereotypes, others on observations of "the way things seem to be." Some are about lesbians, some are about gay men, others are about bi and transgender people – but all of them are very real questions real people have.

Within these pages are opportunities to laugh, poke a little fun, and make each other blush. There are also things I *know* will bring up issues and emotions, so I'd like to offer a few ground rules before you proceed:

- **Only ask the questions you are ready to hear the answers to.** Just because it's in the book doesn't mean you have to ask.

- **Only answer the questions you feel comfortable answering.** It's always OK to say, "Nope, that one's private!" or, "I haven't a clue," or, "I'd rather have nostril surgery than tell you that." *If you don't feel you can easily say no to your friend or loved one, please don't use this book.*

- **Channel your inner Emily Post.** If you think about it, most people never have to answer the personal sorts of questions in this book. For example, can you imagine someone asking, "Did anything happen to make you *straight?*" Probably not, unless you're with a bunch of very drunk LesBiGays on Pride day. So if a LesBiGay person is willing to answer these questions, they're saying, essentially, "I'm making an exception for you because I love you and I trust you." Which is really cool. Respect that trust by setting a clear time and place for your conversation. Adirondack chairs on the porch after dinner? Bud Lights at the corner bar? When the time is up, decide together if you want to continue, or move on to salacious family gossip instead.

- **Remember that the point is not to get everyone to agree, but to understand.** The world is a lot more boring when people always agree with one another anyway. In other words, *Queer Questions Straight Talk* is for you and your loved one or friend if you both feel ready to have the conversation. If your loved one seems more interested in a game of Parcheesi, and uses this book as a drink coaster instead, go with it. Just by offering the opportunity you've still let them know that you're there, that you love them, and you want to talk about it. Believe me, this counts for a whole lot.

Really? You're asking *that*?

You'll notice that there are a number of questions here that seem critical or challenging of LesBiGay people, or based on controversial stereotypes. In addition, there are questions here that LesBiGay people have heard a thousand times and wish would just go away. Here's an example (and the #1 most frequent question I heard in my random polling): "Which one are you, the man or the woman?" Even a gay man festooned in fuchsia and Prada scarves is likely to reply with an annoyed, "We're both the man, thank you very much."

So why am I including these sorts of questions in the book? Because people really seem to want to know the answers. When I solicited questions for this book, I had a lot of straight friends say, "I know I should probably know the answer to this, but..." or, "I hope it's not offensive, but I always wanted to know..." So it looks like we've still got a lot of talking to do with each other.

I'm also a big fan of free speech (old civil rights lawyers never die). I think honest talk is always a good thing as long as everyone remembers a little common courtesy. As your self-appointed guide into this brave new world, I'm instructing everyone to keep the eye-rolling to a minimum. If something in this book makes you want to guffaw, then share with each other what's so damn funny. If you flat out disagree with the very premise of the question, take the opportunity to explain why. The point is to talk. Kindly, respectfully, lovingly.

Aren't you leaving out the "T"?

You have probably heard or used the term "LGBT" or some similar collection of letters. This stands for Lesbian, Gay, Bisexual and Transgender.* You might be wondering if I will be offering questions for transgender (or "trans") people and their loved ones. I will, indeed. Trans people and LesBiGays both challenge conventional ideas about gender, and I believe this is the root of much of our struggle to be accepted. Similarly, lots of LesBiGay people are blurring the

---

*Sometimes you'll see more names in the list: Queer, Questioning, Two Spirit, Intersex and even a few more! – all with specific and important meaning to people in those groups.

distinction between a gay identity and a transgender identity. I will be including some questions about that. However,
the main reason I'm talking primarily about LesBiGays here
is because I frankly don't have enough experience with the
transgender community to represent it as fully as it deserves.
I also believe that there are enough very trans-specific questions to fill up a whole new book. (I would love to see a
"Trans Talk" version come out soon! If you want to write
one, call me, we'll talk.)

Queer Answers

As I was soliciting questions for *Queer Questions Straight
Talk*, I received a number of "queer answers," to go with
them. I'm struck by how many different, thought-provoking
responses there are to any one question. It reminds me
that everyone's journey is unique (either that, or that "gay
agenda" we've heard so much about is really, really long
and contradicts itself all over the place). So, here and there
you'll find some of those answers and other thoughts. Some
are verbatim, others are composites of similar responses I've
heard over and over (names have been changed, except
when otherwise requested). If you find yourself thinking, I
don't agree with any of these people, then great! Fabulous!
Write your own queer answers and send them back to me.

I will post them on my website, and keep the conversation going. www.QueerQuestionsStraightTalk.com

As you peruse this book together, I have one more suggestion for you: relax. Really. Talking about this stuff should be a good – even fun – experience, not excruciating or soul wrenching. In the end it's about love, right?

Oh, and I almost forgot: enjoy the conversation!

Identity

The only queer people are those who don't love anybody.

– Rita Mae Brown

What does it mean when your friend says he's gay? Or when your sister says she's a lesbian? Or bi? If all you ever heard about lesbian or gay people came from the morning news, you'd be tempted to think that there are simply two kinds of people in the world: the straight ones and the gay ones. Ya either are or ya aren't, no waffling in the middle or moving back and forth. Bi people? well . . . they're either confused or celebrities.

I can understand why some people think this way. It's just easier to keep track of things when we've got them neatly organized. And we all like to know where people stand. Are you a Democrat or a Republican? Lefty or Righty? USC or

UCLA ("Michigan or Ohio State!" my partner, Traci, chimes in from the other room)? Boy or Girl? Straight or Gay?

But of course few things in life are this cut and dried. The whole gay/straight dichotomy breaks down pretty quickly when a man who's been apparently happily married for 40 years suddenly runs off with his old army buddy. Or when your roommate from college, the most outspoken lesbian you ever knew, has invited you over to meet her new boy-friend. Let's make it even more complicated: remember when Chastity Bono came out as a lesbian? She's a man now. And a straight one at that.

I had a friend in law school who insisted she was a les-bian and got really impatient with the suggestion that she was anything else – but she only ever dated men, as far as I could tell. Then again, I can think of two bi friends who have never, in all the years I've known them, dated someone of the opposite sex. I've even heard from a few folks who say they're sexually attracted to one sex, but more emotionally attracted to the other. Seems awfully inconvenient, but I'm guessing that people usually find a way to make it all work out.

Are these folks lying? Are they delusional? Are they just trying to make things more confusing? I'm pretty sure the answer is *no* in most cases. More likely, it's that we humans are complicated little beings, with hearts, bodies and minds off exploring and discovering, and perhaps wandering off in all different directions.

Life takes us places we never could have imagined. Just when you thought you could count on some basic things, they up and change on you. Only when we look back do we see clearly the path that brought us to this moment right now. All the while, most of us are doing our very best to be true to ourselves and our loved ones. If you and your loved one are reading this book together, I know you are

The name of the rose

To make sense of it all, we try to name things, to put them in their correct slot. Names matter to people, they give us strength and, yes, identity. This is especially true if you happen to have an identity that the world isn't so enthusiastic about embracing.

To put it more simply, if you don't name yourself, someone else will. I, for example, am a lesbian – not in a phase, not experimenting, not waiting for the right guy. A lesbian. I'm also a Beatles nut, a frequent flier, a failed singer, a lawyer, a daughter and a loyal friend. All of these are identities that add up to me. I've got names for all those parts, but as you and I know, those names can only tell you so much about who a person is.

Right about now, you might be thinking back to high school Shakespeare – by any other name, isn't a rose still a rose? A lesbian still a lesbian? Does it really matter what you call yourself?

Names are funny this way. It is a powerful, frightening, liberating, exciting thing to stand up and declare oneself LesBiGay within a culture that doesn't yet want us to stand up and be counted. To anyone who has ever done this in any setting, let me give you a big pat on the back for being honest and brave. Yet, when someone says, "I'm gay," "I'm straight," "I'm bi," or "I'm lesbian," they are only telling you a tiny part of their story.

The questions in this chapter are about those stories, and what it means to be lesbian, gay or bi...or none of the above. I recommend starting your conversation as if you're opening the first page of a new book.

There is so much ahead to discover.

Questions

Do you think you were always gay or lesbian or bi?

(submitted by the wonderful comic and writer Carol Leifer. Thank you, Carol!)

—m

Do/did you ever wish you were straight?

Did you choose to be LesBiGay? Do you think
it matters if it is or isn't a choice?

—⚏—

Do you think life is harder because you're
LesBiGay than if you were straight?
If so, in what ways?

—⚏—

Do you feel like there's something special
that comes with being LesBiGay?

What the heck am I supposed to call you?
Gay, lesbian, queer, bi, transgender,
questioning? And is it the *LGBT* community,
GLBT ...or *what*? Can you help me
understand why it's so important to
label yourself like this?

—·—

If you haven't had much experience with
the opposite sex, how do you know
you're really LesBiGay?

Do you think of yourself as butch, femme... or none of the above? And what does that mean, anyway?

"I'm a 'tweener. You can call me a bemme, or maybe a *futch*." – Anita

"I think of myself as a woman – and I don't understand why anyone would want to date a woman who didn't act like a woman, or vice versa." – LaVonne

"Butch in the streets, femme in the sheets!" – Terry

Would you be open to a relationship with
someone of the opposite sex?

—w—

What's makes someone LesBiGay, versus trans?
What about a lesbian who is really masculine
or a gay man who is really feminine:
LesBiGay or trans?

—w—

Do you feel you are part of a LesBiGay
community? Where do you feel more
comfortable – with other LesBiGays or
with a mix of people?

Aren't you too young to know you're LesBiGay?

Does anyone ever ask a kid if they're too young to know if they're straight?   – Justin

I've felt this way since I can remember, so I'm pretty sure I'm right about this!   – Sarah

"I guess I'm open to the possibility of a relationship with a girl, but so far I've just been attracted to boys."   – Tyler

Could I have done anything to keep you
from being LesBiGay? Is there anything
I can do about it now?

—◊—

Do you ever question your sexual orientation?
Do you think this could be a phase?

2

Coming Out

There is something about a closet that makes a skeleton terribly restless.

– Wilson Mizner, American playwright

If you remember the 80s, or love all things retro, the term "coming out" might evoke an image of someone throwing the closet door open and dancing into the room to the disco thump of Diana Ross. It's often got an air of joyful fabulousness, as if one were wearing all drab colors one day and then discovered neon and sparkles the next. Did you know that there is even an official Coming Out Day? It's October 11. I like to take the opportunity to call someone who knows me well and announce, "I'm gay!" To which they usually respond, "Um, OK. I was at your gay wedding, remember?" Or if I'm feeling lazy, I just tell my mother...again.

This could make one think that for LesBiGays the world over, Life can be divided into two neat parts: *Life Before*

Coming Out (BCO) and *Life After Coming Out* (ACO) – the BCO era marked by awkward prom photos and futile attempts at dating the guys or gals their parents tried to fix them up with; the ACO era filled with rainbow flags and that spiky haircut (if she's a woman) or really expensive jeans (if he's a man). Oh, that it were that simple!

LesBiGays who have been "out" for a while often look back bemusedly at our earlier lives as a time of desperate but doomed struggle to make heterosexuality fit comfortably – kind of like a pair of pants that's just never going to zip all the way up. If we've been lucky enough to live fairly peacefully as out-in-the-open LesBiGays, we tend to forget an old adage that still applies, and sneaks up just when we think there's no more coming out to do: no matter how far in or out of the closet you are, you still have a next step. It is a process, changing and refining itself every day as we learn who we are and how the world will treat us. This is true for every one of us.

Years ago – I mean in the days of parachute pants and De Loreans – I came out in a great whoosh of nervous excitement. It was the inevitable result of finally freeing something I thought I'd have to keep bottled up ever since I noticed my special fondness for the Bionic Woman in sixth grade (you're doing the math, I can tell). When I realized that maybe I didn't have to keep it all inside forever and ever, I became a veritable lesbian crusader, proudly proclaiming myself to everyone: my mom, my sister, on lesbian and gay speakers' panels, on all the Los Angeles networks covering the local Pride parades. But when I say "everyone," I mean everyone I felt comfortable telling.

I'm totally out...sorta.

It was a lot easier coming out to a classroom full of strangers at the community college than it was to tell my own father. I can't really say why, except that I was still a little embarrassed and even worried that he wouldn't know how to react to me. He finally figured it out on his own ten years later, and as it happened he was perfectly fine about it. In fact, he said that it explained some things about me he never could work out – the lack of a boyfriend being the most obvious one. And I didn't even tell my grandparents until just a few years ago. I thought I was protecting them from feeling uncomfortable or worried about me. Rightly or wrongly, I made that choice for them. (Pondering this with a friend one day, I said that I felt guilty about being dishonest. She let me off the hook with a gentle, "When it comes to family, the normal rules don't apply." I expect that's true for a lot of things we go through.)

As you can see, because life and relationships are always a bit complicated, coming out isn't just something that happens one day and then it's over. LesBiGays are always coming out in one way or another. And think about it: we live in a world where the default setting is always heterosexual. If that's not you, then you've got to (nicely, I hope) tell folks that you are not actually heterosexual. Or choose to stay silent. Medical forms ask for your spouse's name. The office invites spouses to the annual holiday party. If you have kids, people will naturally be curious about their mom and dad. If you went to Disneyworld on your vacation, people will ask you, "Who'd you go with?" Chances are, your answer will be a coming-out opportunity. It's just the way it goes. Even Ellen DeGeneres must still have moments in her life when she comes out to someone – and arguably no one is more out than Ellen.

I've been lucky. By and large, I have been treated well by my family and friends and even strangers. In fact, most of the time when I've worried that someone would have a hard time knowing, I've been surprised instead by their support. Even so, I've experienced real pain and misunderstanding when I least expected it. I have had my identity questioned and outright dismissed at times both by strangers and people I love. I've been psychoanalyzed by people who know nothing about me, been called a sinner and a pervert and even physically threatened when I have held another woman's hand in public. So maybe it's not surprising that even as a public lesbian in many arenas, there are still situations when I choose to stay in the closet – sometimes for very good reasons. While I've found that the vast majority of people are sweet and respectful, there are times when I'm not at all confident that I will be safe and comfortable if people know.

The choice to come out is not a choice between being gutsy or wussy – let me be very clear about this. Many of us do not live in families, towns or countries, or work in jobs, where it is always safe to be openly LesBiGay. Often, many of us just don't yet know if we will be greeted warmly, coolly, outright rejected...or worse. To come out is, ultimately, a very personal decision with high stakes. For the most part, I advise against pressuring *anyone* to come out, even if they are so obviously "on the team" they ought to be on the back cover of this book.

That's fine, honey...just don't tell Dad.

Coming out isn't just for LesBiGays either. Every parent, child, sibling or friend of LesBiGay has his or her own coming out decisions to make. What do you tell folks at work when they ask if your son is married? What do you say to your neighbors when they recognize your mom dancing on a float at the Pride parade on the evening news? Just about every LesBiGay has heard the words some time or another, "I'm fine with it, but don't tell so-and-so, it will *kill* them." As tempting as it might be for LesBiGays to say, "I'll tell whoever I want!" I suggest a little patience and understanding here instead. Perhaps a better approach is to ask about why in fact so-and-so will keel over dead from the shock and see instead if it's only a straight loved one's own coming-out jitters. It can be intimidating to everyone at first.

Do I have to do this again?

At its best, this constant decision making about if and when it's time to come out can be tiring – for straight people and LesBiGays alike. Each person will work out his or her own process for coming out. For me, I got so weary of always having to stop and declare myself that at some point I decided to skip the process entirely and carry on as if people already knew. Now my answer to the question, "What are you doing for Thanksgiving?" might be, "Oh, we're going to my partner's parents'. Her mom is famous for her pink Jell-O salad."

While I do suggest that a gentle push against the closet door does one good on a regular basis, I can't emphasize enough that coming out is a delicate, personal judgment call, unique to each of us. So as you talk about the questions in this chapter, remember that coming out is a journey more than a single act. Rarely does it unfold in a straight line, but with a little luck every LesBiGay will carry with him or her a bit of common sense and wisdom and, I hope so very much, a strong sense of personal pride. The questions in this chapter might very well be an important part of that journey.

Enjoy the conversation along the way.

Questions

Were you worried I wouldn't understand?

—ᴍ—

What kinds of things go through your mind
when you consider coming out to someone?
Are you ever nervous, excited, afraid?

Does this mean I won't have grandkids?

—⚭—

How should I talk to someone who I'm pretty sure is LesBiGay, but hasn't told me yet? Do I tell them that I know, pretend that they're straight, or avoid the subject until they tell me?

—⚭—

Do you have to tell everyone? Do I have to tell everyone too?

Comic Michele Balan answers the question:

"When did you first know?
How did you know?"

I grew up in the 1970s, a decade of peace, love, and rock and roll, but not an openly gay decade. I didn't know what gay was. I recall going out with boys because that was what I was expected to do. I would kiss my boyfriend and wonder why I didn't feel happy or excited. I thought maybe it was just the boyfriend, so I would get a new one, and still no excitement. Then one day I was in the backseat of a car with my boyfriend, while one of my good friends was in the front seat making out with her boyfriend. As I was watched them kiss I finally got excited. But it wasn't from kissing my boyfriend, it was from watching my girlfriend kiss hers! Of course, my boyfriend had no idea that and he was benefiting from my little bit of voyeurism.

I went home that night and thought, What's wrong with me...some kind of disease? I actually thought it was a sickness. I didn't know who to talk to, because in those days there weren't LGBT groups in school, or gay characters on TV I could identify with. I became a lonely and unhappy teenager that smoked a lot of pot, LSD, and even more. I used drugs to ease the pain. Now I was really a mess: a gay drug addict! So for me, it wasn't as simple as just waking up one day and realizing I was gay.

I've come across some people who are so androgynous I can't tell if they're male or female. How do I find out? Does this mean that they're LesBiGay? Trans? What pronouns should I use?

—∞—

Is there anyone you haven't told yet but would like to? What's stopping you?

—∞—

Why does it suddenly seem like everybody and their dogs are declaring themselves LesBiGay?

What's the funniest thing that's happened when you've told someone? Have your friends told you any outrageous coming-out stories?

—⟋⟍—

How can I tell whether someone is LesBiGay?

"She has every song Melissa Etheridge ever recorded, including the rare b-sides (and she tells you she's a lesbian). He loves Judy Garland and broadway shows (and he tells you he's gay). He seems really, really close to his bowling buddies (and he tells you he's bi)." – Phoenix

"Even if you're pretty sure, you can never really know until that person decides to tell you." – Jocelyn

Actress and Director Amanda Bearse answers the question:

"When did you tell your daughter you were gay?"

This was an interesting question once posed to me by one of the parents in my daughter's preschool. Zoe was adopted at birth and so by this time she was about four years old. I had blended families with my lesbian partner and her daughter and we had been living together as a family for several years, all of which was familiar to this parent. So I paused, thinking of the best way to answer her because frankly, she was quite a kind person and very earnest in her desire to know. I said, "Your husband is a doctor, right?" She nodded her head yes. I continued, "So when did you tell your son he had a doctor for a father? Did you sit him down one day and explain it, or did he just understand that being a doctor was a part of who his father was in the world?" She got what I was saying and smiled.

As LGBT people, our love, our loving relationships, within our homes and often shared with (our) children, is as inherent and "normal" and "seen and known" as any straight couple's would be. It's that's simple.

3

Stereotypes

You're born naked, the rest is drag.

– RuPaul

Even the most polite and thoughtful among us stereotype people. It's a natural instinct to help us identify folks and know where to begin the conversation. If I'm at a party and want to break the ice with a man who has a tattoo on his neck and a shark's tooth through his septum, I probably won't ask him if he scrapbooks. Likewise, I won't ask the 90-year-old woman in line at the post office if that's her chopper blocking my car outside. This is stereotyping – and quite possibly, I would be wrong in both cases. If I am, the consequences are not too great: a little embarrassment, and maybe an apology to the senior division of my local Hell's Angels chapter.

When it comes to stereotyping minority groups, things become riskier. At best, it's impolite and makes it look like we get all our information from old TV shows. At worst, stereotyping dehumanizes people, reducing them to caricatures – something to be derided or dismissed. All through history stereotyping has been the key component of prejudice and bigotry. All through history, too, stereotypes have eventually been proven wrong.

Because of this, I can imagine that lots of straight people are hesitant to ask about the inexplicable things that LesBi-Gays do, so as not to cause offense. In most circumstances I'd applaud such restraint. The problem is, frankly, that lots of LesBiGays do things that seem really, really gay – and straight people just don't get it. If you've ever seen *RuPaul's Drag Race* on the Logo channel, you'll understand what I mean – some things need a bit of explaining. But it can be a lot of pressure to put on one LesBiGay person, to represent the opinions, tastes and preferences of LesBiGays the world over; we can be just as much at a loss to explain some things as a straight person.

There's probably no better use for a few Queer Questions than trying to make sense of stereotypes. To get started, I'll let you in on a little secret: LesBiGays stereotype one another all the time.

Gaydar or...

I'm sure you've heard of *gaydar*, that legendary skill we LesBiGays are reported to have that allows us to identify one another with a mere glance. While you and your loved one may debate its existence or accuracy, let me offer one school of thought: Gaydar, at least in part, is just stereotyping with inside information.

But it doesn't always work as planned. Here's an example: Some time ago I thought I had my gaydar so well calibrated that I could peg every LesBiGay within a 100 yards of me wherever I was. Then I went to Amsterdam. There, I quickly discovered that my criteria for conclusively identifying whether someone was as gay as a *Golden Girls* Fanfest lined up nearly identically with the general physical description of a Dutch person. Spiky platinum 'do and funky bohemian glasses? Lesbian...or Dutch. Sculpted cheekbones, "manpris"(capris for men), and leather messenger bag? Gay...or Dutch. In fact, my LesBiGay stereotypes so completely broke down in most parts of Northern Europe I visited that I found myself utterly unable to spot my own kind anywhere in my travels. Everyone seemed LesBiGay to me.

I learned an important lesson on my trip: that there is, of course, a lot more to being LesBiGay (or European) than our favorite stereotypes. Chances are I can pick some of us out of a crowd based on my stereotypes. Chances are equally good that I'll snag a few European tourists (LesBiGay or otherwise) in my net as well, and that I'll miss a whole lot more LesBiGays who don't fit my limited preconceptions.

The obvious and then some

The stereotypes aren't necessarily wrong, they're just not all that meaningful on their own. There's also so much more to find out about people. Think of it like this: if you see a man out your office window who is practically sashaying down the street, you will likely guess that he's gay (I would too, so don't worry). It's what comes afterwards that matters. You could just file him away under the heading, GAY, and let it go at that. Or you could think, "Hmm. I wonder why he's sashaying today. Has he come out of the closet at last and now he's dancing along in a dizzying new flush of liberation? Is he practicing for a show? Does he do this every day or is this a one-time thing? What's the story?" Now, I don't recommend dropping your lunch, running outside and peppering a stranger with all these questions, but I do suggest keeping an open and inquiring mind. If you're right, and he's gay, there's more to find out before you really know anything about this guy. And he could be straight.

It's nice to be confused by stereotypes sometimes. I love the fact that my one of my favorite people in the world, a big, butch straight-as-they-come fireman, is as proud and out loud as he can be about his two gay uncles who partly raised him. I love listening to the swaggering lesbian couple at the nursery debating the pros and cons of rose colors for their garden. I love it when my swishy gay male friend insists on opening doors for me and acting like Cary Grant when we go out together. There is room for all of us to surprise one another and transcend the stereotypes, which can be kind of sweet and fun. It doesn't mean that there's no truth to the stereotypes, but that the obvious things become way more complex and nuanced upon further observation – and that's when it gets really interesting.

So go ahead and ask your loved one what's the deal with all that Dykes-on-Bikes stuff or all those gay hairdressers, but remember that just when you think you've got someone pegged, you've closed the door to finding out more.

Enjoy the conversation and be ready for some answers you didn't expect at all!

Questions

Is one of you the "man" and one the "woman"?

—∿—

Do all LesBiGays have "gaydar"?

—∿—

Do you think that more straight people could
be at least bi if they were just open to it?

Why do lesbians I meet seem so, well, masculine? If they're just like every other gal, why do the ones I see do things like wear ties and a mullet?

—∿—

Did something happen to you to make you LesBiGay?

—∿—

Are there any real lesbians like the ones on the *L Word*?

Why do gay guys I meet seem so, well,
effeminate? If they're just like every
other guy, why do the ones I see do things
like wear eyeliner and watch
America's Next Top Model?

—⁂—

I've heard that some transsexuals are also
LesBiGay – i.e., a straight man who
transitions into a woman and then keeps
dating women. How can that be?

—⁂—

Are lesbians angry at men? Are gay men angry
at women? Are bi people angry at anyone?

Why does it seem like all lesbians have cats
and gay men have little matching dogs?

"That's a total stereotype...although
I do have 3 cats." – Andrea

"A good gay man would never have
ordinary mismatched mutts." – Geoffrey

Why do so many LesBiGays like performers
like Lady Gaga, Cher and Bette Midler?
What's so LesBiGay about them?

Why are so many lesbians handy with tools?

—⚮—

What's dressing in drag all about? Do most
gay men like to do it? What about lesbians
and bi folks?

—⚮—

What happens in gay bars? Can
straight people go there?

—⚮—

What's the deal with gay guys calling each
other *Mary* or *girlfriend* or *her*. Do lesbians
call each other *Bob* and *dude* and *him*?

Why does it seem like LesBiGays often want to shock straight people – like being outrageous at Gay Pride parade and/or dressing in drag? Doesn't this hurt how people view you?

—∭—

Is it true that Suburus are lesbians' favorite cars? Why???

—∭—

Are bi people more likely to be promiscuous? Or are they just unwilling to commit?

How can I make sure LesBiGay people don't hit on me?

"Well, if you keep wearing Dockers and Hawaiian shirts, I can guarantee no man will hit on you. But seriously, if you're not interested, just say no...just like straight people do with each other." – Josh

"This makes me think about my dad who would never go to the obviously gay hairdresser back in my home town. One day I said, 'Dad, trust me, you are totally safe with Stephen. I can assure you that he doesn't want you. You are as straight as they come.' I think maybe Dad thought that he'd get hit on just because he's a guy. (Love you, Dad.)"
– Traci (your author's ever-patient partner)

4

Marriage & Relationships

Of course I believe in gay marriage —
why shouldn't they have to suffer just like us straight couples do?
— *Dolly Parton*

When I came out way back when, LesBiGays had only one term for that special person: my lover. It always made me cringe a little, since it seemed so very personal to, say, go to the grocery store and tell the cashier that my lover is outside picking up two bags of ice from the freezer and can we add that to the bill, please. It also made my mother pray fervently for some other word every time she had to say something like, "And are you having your new...ah...lover here for dinner?"

Back then, when LesBiGays announced, "This is my lover!" it meant we weren't just good friends, if you know what I mean. But it reflected, too, our sense of joy and triumph that we could have a romantic relationship at all – openly, proudly, and without necessarily getting investigated by the FBI because of it.

What a sign of the times that hardly anyone says it anymore. And it's not because we've marched back into the closet. Nor is it because our most intimate desires and dreams have really changed much. Now we say, my husband, my wife, my partner, my spouse, my guy, my gal, my lady (shudder). We're on a veritable roll to find that perfect name for the person we love. The broader culture seems to have gotten a lot more comfortable with the idea that LesBiGays are looking for the same things in a relationship that everyone else is: love, commitment, family dinners, TV in bed, and even kids. OK, some LesBiGay people – just like straights – couldn't imagine any worse hell than a cupboard full of sippy cups and a split-level in the 'burbs. I confess that I enter a kind of wide-eyed paralysis when my friends' toddlers, covered in something gooey and blue, rush me while screaming exuberantly, "Aunt Abby!" I love 'em, but...

This is why marriage (with or without the blue goo) has become front and center in the lesbian and gay rights movement. For many of us, marriage is the gold standard. Anything less is a constant reminder that our love doesn't rate. Just a few decades back, when even couples who'd been together 70 years were still calling each other, sweetly, "my lover," we couldn't imagine that today we'd be demanding – and expecting – this particular kind of equality.

You'll notice I said, "many of us" in the paragraph above. Not everyone dreams of a storybook wedding. For some LesBiGays, our relationships are something wonderfully different and mold-breaking. Why be lockstep with everyone else when we've already scared the horses?

Getting to the heart of marriage

When my partner Traci asked me to marry her, I had to think long and hard about what marriage actually meant to me. It had always seemed to be something based in rigid gender roles – guys in tuxes, women in white, virginal taffeta – and that didn't make sense for us at all. I thought about the history of marriage, where until pretty recently it was an economic and political arrangement, rarely having to do with love or equality. To say yes, and really mean it, I needed to imagine something new, an image of marriage that made sense for Traci and me.

After much thought, the most simple answer came: marriage meant that we, she and I, would be family. No more, no less.

I said yes, eventually, and we planned our wedding, compromising on a few points (she conceded that we didn't need a reception at the Moose Lodge, I let go of the Beatles tribute band idea), but agreeing completely that by getting married we were affirming that we were family, with all that that entails. How radical, and yet how traditional.

I'm sure, whether you're gay, lesbian, bi or straight, this doesn't sound so very different from your own thought process around love and marriage (or no marriage at all), which is exactly the idea. All romantic relationships are unique, something we learn and create as we go. So, as you browse through the questions in this chapter, keep two things in the back of your mind: first, it's been a long, hard struggle – one that is far from over – for LesBiGays to be able to live and love in peace; and second, that's all anybody wants anyway.

Enjoy the conversation!

Questions

How do you know that someone you're
interested in is LesBiGay too?

—⚭—

What's your perfect date like?

—⚭—

Do you have a crush on anyone right now
that you haven't told me about yet?

Do you want to have kids?

—∿—

Do you worry that your kids would be
stigmatized because they have LesBiGay
parents? How would you deal with that?

—∿—

What's the most challenging thing about having
a relationship with someone of the same sex?

—∿—

Is having a marriage ceremony important
to you? What's the difference between that
and a commitment ceremony?

What's the best thing about being involved with someone of the same sex?

"Sharing clothes!" – Alyssa

"We're both from Mars." – Ryan

"I completely understand her PMS." – Nicole

Where do you go to meet other LesBiGay people...at bars, on the Internet, at work?

Are there different issues that come up in LesBiGay relationships than in straight relationships?

—⁓—

How should I introduce your partner to other people?

—⁓—

There are lots of LesBiGay parents nowadays – do you think this will make their kids LesBiGay too?

If you had a child, how would you feel if he
or she turned out to be LesBiGay?

—∞—

Do I need to worry about my kids being
around LesBiGays?

—∞—

How do children of LesBiGay couples
address their parents –
Dad and Daddy, Mom and Mommy?

Do you think that being exposed to LesBiGay relationships, or images of them in the media, will make kids more likely to experiment with LesBiGay behavior?

—⁂—

Why do lesbians so often stay friends with their exes? Do gay men do this too?

—⁂—

I know a lot of straight women have gay best friends. Do straight men have lesbian best friends, too? What's the best thing about friendships like these?

If my son likes to play dress up does that mean he's going to be gay?

"I don't know, but if that's what he wants let him be free to play how he wants!" – Paula

"No, it might just mean he'll have good fashion sense." – Martin

"Maybe – or he might be transgender."
– Darlene

5

Homophobia & Politics

*Everything that irritates us about others
can lead us to an understanding of ourselves.*

– Carl Jung

By reading this far, you're already making the world a better, kinder place for LesBiGays. If you weren't quite thinking on that big a scale at the moment, this might surprise
you, but you are indeed creating change. You might even be
putting an end to homophobia.

A lot of people take exception to the word "homophobia"
because it literally means (from Greek) "fear of the same,"
which doesn't totally make sense. First of all, it seems a more
apt label for someone who, say, has a problem with things in
pairs, like socks, cops and sweater sets. Another reasonable-
but-not-ideal interpretation might be "fear of homos," rather

than the more accurate-but-clunky "fear of people who have an affinity for people of the same sex."

Second, I've heard some dedicated homophobes say things like, "I'm not afraid of them, I just don't like 'em!" Fair enough, I suppose – but when people start acting on that dislike it can look a whole lot like they are, in fact, afraid of us.

The third reason some people have a hard time with the word is that it seems like an awfully loaded and judgmental label to describe their own uncertainty and discomfort around LesBiGays. This makes sense, as there is so much confusing information and political rhetoric out there about us. As with the terms racist! and sexist!, it's pretty easy to hurl the label homophobe! at someone who is in the early stages of simply trying to understand. What a way to shut someone up real quick. And that's not what this book's about.

I should tell you, however, that homophobia is very real for every LesBiGay. Indulge me for a moment to talk about how homophobia can affect us.

The subtle and not-so-subtle

Regardless of whether or not our loved ones and communities are accepting of us as LesBiGays, homophobia in the larger culture is always creeping around in the background somewhere. On a good day, homophobia exists as a nagging stressor – the thing that happens every time someone assumes in casual conversation that there's not a woman on this planet who would kick George Clooney out of bed for eating saltines, and that all men dream of a girl like Pamela Anderson (this even annoys quite a few straight men I know who lean more towards brains or booty).

Homophobia even exists in the fact that *Dancing With the Stars* will never pair one of their delightful male dance pros with…um…Peyton Manning. (But wouldn't you pay good money to see that? I sure would.) Like everyone else, LesBiGays aren't expecting anything different, but every once in a while many of us sigh and wonder why we can't see our lives reflected back to us a little more in the world we all inhabit.

And then there are those days when homophobia is the thing that knocks the wind right out of our sails. Imagine that you're shopping at Target, going to church, waving goodbye to your child on the school bus, and making plans for you and the people that you call family – and it's gotten some total stranger's knickers in a Gordian knot. This is how a lot of us felt in recent times, when various organizations raised unprecedented amounts of money and ire to fight same-sex marriage in several states. As a civil rights lawyer I'll grudgingly concede that everyone is entitled to express his or her own opinion, but what stunned so many of us LesBiGays was just how much we suddenly felt like the scariest people on the planet. Oh, I would love to have as much power as Pat Robertson says I do!

The painful politics of shutting doors and shutting up

Let me up the ante a little more: homophobia is what keeps people locked in the closet so they don't lose their jobs or get kicked out of their family home. Homophobia can make someone lose custody of their own children, or never have the right to adopt the child they raised from infancy with their partner. Homophobia can break sweethearts apart, cause isolation and depression, lead to increased risk of alcoholism, drug use and, for some, suicide (LesBiGay teens are up to four times more likely to attempt suicide than straight teens, and LesBiGay teens from homes that reject them are *eight* times more likely). Those of us who don't have to face these sorts of issues every day feel lucky or blessed, but none of us can ever forget what the stakes really are for living our lives freely.

You can't talk about all this stuff without also talking about politics. For example, until just a few years ago, same-sex sex was illegal in a number of states. The police could peek in your bedroom window and arrest you…really. Things have changed some, but the laws are still all over the map.

Let me just give a brief status report on LesBiGay rights in the U.S. right now:

- There are no federal laws protecting LesBiGays from employment discrimination.

- There are no federal laws that recognize same-sex civil unions or partnerships of any kind – let alone marriage.

- As of this writing, five states recognize same-sex marriage. Many years ago in Hawaii, and more recently in California and Maine, courts recognized the right, but voters rescinded it.

- The majority of states have outright bans on same-sex marriage, while a minority of states recognize some form of civil union or domestic partnership.

- Laws prohibiting employment and housing discrimination vary markedly among the states and municipalities – from no protection at all to full equality.

- LesBiGay people are prohibited from serving in the U.S. Armed Forces (since 1994, approximately 13,000 servicemen and women have been discharged under the Don't Ask Don't Tell policy).

Outside of the U.S., the political status of LesBiGays varies from almost total equality to downright medieval. For example, same-sex marriage is recognized in places as varied as Canada, Norway, South Africa and Mexico City. Meanwhile, gay men in Iraq are being chased and tortured to death by religious edict in certain areas, and Uganda is considering a law that makes homosexuality punishable by death and requires people to notify the officials if they merely know anyone who is gay, lesbian or bisexual.

Looking for a cure

I don't mean to be such a downer here, because I believe there is hope. The cure for homophobia, according to me, is communication. This is what you are doing now: being brave, putting it out there, learning and listening. You and your loved one may never see eye to eye on anything from same-sex marriage to AIDS funding policy or sex ed in schools. It's not all that important that you do. What is important is the end of misinformation about who LesBiGays are and a willingness for straight and LesBiGay people alike to tell our stories – to each other and to the world around us.

I have total faith in you.

Questions

What's the most important thing you want
straight people to understand about LesBiGays?

—✕—

Has anyone done anything threatening or
scary to you because you're LesBiGay?

—✕—

How does it feel to hear words like dyke,
faggot, or queer?

Should LesBiGays have special rights?

—∾—

Are bi people less stigmatized than gays
or lesbians?

—∾—

Kate Kendell (Executive Director of
the National Center for Lesbian Rights)
answers the question:

Is there a gay agenda, and if so, what is it?

"This is an easy one. The 'gay agenda' is the agenda
of every single person in America: to live fully and
freely – to enjoy equality under the law – to not
fear or be shamed by who you are. It's an agenda
of human rights and basic freedom."

Don't some of your LesBiGay rights step on
my own right to live according to
my personal beliefs?

—៣—

How are transgender issues the same as
(or different from) LesBiGay issues?

—៣—

With all the other problems in the world right
now, can't LesBiGay rights wait a bit? Is it really
as important as things like poverty and
global warming and racism?

What's one thing I could do to support you –
to be an ally?

—⁓—

What do you think of "outing" public figures
who are in the closet?

"I think coming out is an important and
empowering personal experience –
there's no excuse for denying someone
the right to choose when and how
they do it."   – Danielle

"If someone is using their fame or power to
keep gay people down, then they should be
exposed for the hypocrites they are."   – Aaron

What's your response to the argument
that if we allow same-sex marriage then
we're on a slippery slope to people
marrying goats, etc?

—◊◊—

What is your response to the argument that
domestic partnership is good enough and that
marriage should be saved for men and women?

—◊◊—

What do you think about the Don't Ask Don't Tell
policy in the military or the Boy Scouts' ban
on gay members?

A personal question from Paul Tagliabue, former Commissioner of the NFL:

My son's partner is from Australia and faces unique immigration law issues because he is part of a same-sex couple. So my question for my son, his partner and other people like them, is this:

"Because the U.S. won't recognize same-sex partners from abroad the same way it recognizes opposite-sex spouses, how did it feel to find out you had to choose between love and country?"

Why does it seem like as soon as LesBiGay people make some social progress they keep pushing so hard for more – like gays in the clergy or transgender rights or marriage?

—⁓—

What can I do to make the world a better place for LesBiGays?

"Just listen." – Amy

"Don't be afraid to bring it up with me if you have questions." – Rhianne

"Do more than say you accept me – try to talk to your friends openly and pay attention to what's going on in your community about gay rights." – Luis

6

Religion & Spirituality

God won't let you or me stay put, content to believe
what we've always believed, what we've always been taught,
what we've always assumed.

– *Rt. Rev. V. Gene Robinson, Bishop of New Hampshire*
First openly gay Episcopal bishop

There is perhaps no aspect of LesBiGay identity as challenging for people to get their heads around as spirituality (OK, maybe sex. We'll get to that). It's easy to think of LesBiGay life as existing completely separate from religion, a mistake just everyone makes sometimes, no matter where they are on the continuum of sexuality. And yet there are LesBiGay people in every single faith and denomination on Earth. Every single one.

The profound desire to feel a connection to God, the Universe, Allah or the Creator does not simply vanish because someone is gay. In fact, many spiritual LesBiGay people find that the process of coming out and learning to live authentically only makes their path to the Divine more meaningful. And many owe their very happiness as LesBiGay people to the presence of God in their lives.

But whether communities of faith always welcome LesBiGay people is another question entirely. You'd have to have been living under a rock for the last 20 years if you didn't know about the "culture wars" going on right now between religion and homosexuality. Prominent leaders in all the Western religions (Christianity, Judaism and Islam) have declared homosexuality a sin – or at least a departure from God's best plan, as I've heard the mega-pastor Joel Osteen put it a few times.* And while many other leaders from within each great faith tradition, both in the East and West, have stated just as confidently that LesBiGays should feel right at home in their religious communities, the common perception is that they have few places of worship anywhere in the world that will greet them with anything more than a tight-lipped smile and furtive wink from the organist.

Damned if you do...

With millions of people squawking about the state of the queer soul on TV, pulpits and the Internet, it must seem like

---

*Eastern religions, very generally, are far less concerned with the questions of homosexuality.

the whole world is offering its two cents on one very personal journey. Regardless of your own feelings on the subject, just imagine for a moment what this weight of opinion must feel like to the person who simply wants to find some peace between loving another person in that special way and loving God. On top of that, most people can't easily separate their religious community from their social network, so if they happen to have been raised in a religious community that frowns on homosexuality, they risk losing friends and family right along with any sense of spiritual belonging. I have known quite a few people who have felt quietly ripped in two as they've tried to figure out how to be true to themselves.

This is where I think a conversation about spirituality has got to start, with the understanding that – really – we all just want to feel loved and connected: with a partner, with our families, with our Creator. Who doesn't want this? Even if you're an atheist, life must certainly be a lot sweeter if you feel like you're a beloved part of this whole, crazy spinning ball of stuff we call Earth.

OK, so I get that it might be hard to feel supportive when you are concerned about the very soul of your loved one. Or you might have grave doubts or confusion about how to square what your pastor or rabbi says with what you feel in your heart. Or maybe you just don't get what all the fuss is about and why your loved one (LesBiGay or otherwise) is getting all worked up about it anyway. It's all understandable – like I said, this is a tough and confusing one for a lot of folks. But it's not impossible.

Blessed are the bridge-builders

As I've put together this little book, I've talked with people from a range of Western faith traditions. I noticed that people from wildly different points on the religious compass, from a liberal rabbi to an Alabama-drawl Southern Baptist, expressed some of the same core ideas. I learned that each faith has wonderful tools for building bridges across the deepest divides, but that people tend to forget all about that when they're feeling defensive, tired or worried. So, as you dive into this chapter, keep in mind some of these tips I've heard from a range of religious people:

- ◆ The first is that we all have purpose, our lives have purpose. Gay, straight, bi, or lesbian, it doesn't matter: our lives are gifts, to be handled with compassion, patience and love. We're all trying to get there as best we can.

- ◆ If you believe in "loving the sinner, hating the sin" you can get to the "love" part of things through questions and communication. Remember that being alienated from your family or loved ones is not an ideal that any religion or belief system is about.

◆ Though some religious people interpret scripture more literally than others, religious texts rarely exist in a vacuum. Yes, there are stories about any number of hair-curling sins, yet there are so many more stories about being compassionate, free of judgment, and just, well, nice. Get in touch with these great and loving aspects of your religious tradition.

I'd like to share a verse attributed to the 13th century Sufi poet Rumi. I like it because it reminds me how welcoming and hopeful faith can be.

Come, come, whoever you are.
Wanderer, worshipper, lover of leaving — it doesn't matter,
Ours is not a caravan of despair.
Come, even if you have broken your vow a thousand times,
*Come, come again, come.**

You can interpret these lines many ways, but it's hard to miss that, above all else, the narrator is joyfully offering up love and kindness for the soul that is seeking a place to belong. That's really what it's about, isn't it?

If you find no other common ground but your love for each other, you will have accomplished a lot.

---

*As quoted in *Rumi and His Sufi Path of Love* by M. Fatih Citlak and Huseyin Bingul, Tughra Books, 2007

Questions

Do you believe you can be LesBiGay and
go to Heaven?

—◊◊—

Do you think that God or the Creator made
you this way?

—◊◊—

Do you consider yourself religious or spiritual?
How does being LesBiGay fit into that?

Have you ever prayed to change?

"Yes. Sometimes being gay feels like a burden, tripping me up on my spiritual journey. It would be so much easier if I could just love like everyone else." – Thomas

"I used to pray that I'd be totally straight, but clearly that didn't happen. I do not doubt that God can do all things, but I have to wonder if praying not to be gay is about as useful as praying that I will grow three inches taller or that my eyes will turn blue." – John

"No way. I think being a lesbian has actually been a blessing. I am just thankful I live in a time where I can live openly and worship in a church that feels like home." – Julia

So many religions think LesBiGay people
are going to hell; why would you want to
be a part of any group that would say
that about you?

—⁓—

Since you came out, how has your spiritual/
religious life evolved?

—⁓—

What's been the hardest thing to make peace
with in your religious beliefs?

How do you feel going to the
church/temple/mosque you were brought
up in? Is it welcoming? Annoying?
Scary? Just plain weird?

—∞—

Have you felt rejected by your friends or
members of your family because they
thought you were a sinner?

—∞—

What's the funniest thing (intentional or not)
you've heard anyone say about LesBiGay
people and religion?

How can you be LesBiGay and still call yourself a Christian/Muslim/Jew/etc.? Isn't that totally against Scripture?

"When I die and go to judgment day, my God's going to say that I was gay – and maybe that wasn't so good. On the other hand, I was a good person who lived kindly. Balanced out on the scales of justice, I believe God will give me a thumbs up." – Amir

"I have spent the last 15 years of my life trying to fit in with a spiritual community, and at times I've just been ready to throw in the towel with church all together." – Melissa

"When people say Scripture forbids this, I respond, 'It also says an eye for an eye, but no one does that anymore.' Interpretation of Scripture has to change with the times." – Enrique

Do you feel alienated spiritually from your family and friends? What's that like? What would it take to heal that rift?

—◦◦◦

Have you ever gone to one of those "gay" churches (Metropolitan Community Churches, for example)? What on earth do they talk about?

—◦◦◦—

How can I support you – and accept your partner into my home – when it goes against everything I believe? Aren't you being disrespectful of *me*?

How does it feel when religious leaders say things like "Gay people are trying to destroy the family," or "Gay people caused Hurricane Katrina"?

"Even though I know that a lot of that stuff about gay people isn't true, I worry about what the Bible says about us. I can't just ignore it." – Keenon

"I can't stand the fact that a church that is supposed to be teaching themes of love and acceptance of all people instead adds to the divisiveness of this issue. I'm always afraid that one day someone will come to church seeking comfort who is in a very fragile emotional state and they'll find no support system whatsoever." – Mandy

What am I supposed to tell my friends
at temple/church/mosque when
they ask about you?

"I'm sorry it's so hard for you to talk about me
at church. I try not to feel like you're ashamed
of me, and I instead, I just ask you to take baby
steps. How about telling just one person you
really trust, first?"   – Darren

"Don't even hesitate for a second. Tell 'em your son
is in a great relationship with a lovely man, that
he's happy and healthy and that you're very proud
of him! No one can argue with that."   – Isaiah

"Whatever you do, don't just pretend I'm
something I'm not."   – Gwen

7

Sex

*Science is a lot like sex. Sometimes something useful comes of it,
but that's not the reason we're doing it.*

– Richard Feynman

Sex. It's on everyone's mind – including yours and mine –
but it's probably the hardest thing of all to talk about. I'm
blushing as I write.

I recently met a woman who, right after learning that I was
a lesbian, asked, "You know why people have a hard time
with y'all?" I started to reply, but she cut me off with, "It's
the sex! Not all that political and religious stuff or anything
– just the sex. It freaks people out."

I was tempted to say, "Well, duh," but her gutsy honesty
caused me to bite my tongue and reflect before cracking
wise. She was right, and some part of me had forgotten.
Yes, there are lots of things about LesBiGays that straight

people struggle with. Breaking gender norms is probably the biggest, followed by religious prohibition. But – at the risk of oversimplifying – all of these things become a way bigger deal if you throw sex into the mix.

If my partner and I did everything we normally do together – traveling, bickering over the remote (my obsession with BBC documentaries, her lust for reality shows), eating too much, cleaning the cat box – no one would have a single problem with it. We might be written off as spinster sisters or something similarly dull. But add sex to the list and we are suddenly the hottest, trendiest and most controversial thing around. In some places, same-sex sex is the difference between simply being the town eccentric and getting arrested or assaulted.

Sex, sex and more sex...

I confess that it can get tiresome when some straight people place so much emphasis on our sex lives, as if that were the only thing that defined LesBiGays (and not, say, our penchant for high design or women's rugby). Here's an example:

Quite a while ago, in 1993, Newsweek publicized a study that showed there were far fewer lesbian and gay people in the country than previously estimated.* That was big news because up until then, LesBiGays had been using the even

---

*"How Many Gays are There?" Feb. 15, 1993

older Kinsey Report statistics that 1 in 10 Americans were gay. I devoured the article, fascinated, albeit a little disappointed about our shrinking numbers. Then I noticed something odd: they had defined lesbians and gays as people who had had a sexual encounter with another person of the same sex within the last year. Everybody else, according to Newsweek, was heterosexual, whether or not they'd slept with anyone, ever. (No one was bi in 1993 either, apparently.) Imagine my horror when I realized that these researchers had yanked my lesbian status just because I was going through an extended miserable dating period. No wonder there weren't that many gays around – not everyone gets lucky all the time.

I cite this study because it is still referred to frequently today, continually reinforcing the idea that it's just about sex, sex, sex.

My immediate response to this sort of thinking is that sex defines LesBiGays as much as sex defines heterosexuals. In other words, LesBiGays aren't just all about the sex. A more thoughtful response is that sex does in fact matter. I didn't fall for my partner because of her cooking skills and the insurance benefits I could get through her work – though those are very nice – I fell for her because she was attractive to me. She was beautiful, had great thick hair, a perfect nose, a keen sense of humor and a lovely smell. She also had a nice rack. There, I said it. She does.

This all adds up to sex. Is that all that's between us? Certainly not, but we wouldn't be here now, arguing over whether we watch *American Idol* or a 4-part history of Victorian plumbing if it weren't for all those sex hormones.

So it is important. Is it anyone's else's business? Probably not. But right here, for a little while at least, I'm giving you permission to talk about it and get all that curiosity out in the open. I just have a few tips:

First, it's a good time to remember the guidelines I mentioned in the Intro. It's OK to ask and it's OK to decline to answer. Don't ask the questions if you're not ready for the answers, and don't answer the questions you don't feel comfortable answering. If in doubt, just say, "Next!"

Second, remember that we're all sexual creatures in one way or another. That doesn't necessarily mean that we share the same sexual tastes. In fact, I know we don't. As a dear friend of mine once said (and I even put it on Traci's and my wedding invitations), "There's an ass for every saddle." Try not to worry so much about the details of what people get up to in private. It could just freak you out.

Finally, having said all that, know your personal comfort limits for sharing, and proceed carefully.

I'll leave you with a little anecdote: A few years back, my mom started dating after a period out of the old game. She wanted to talk about it, clearly, but seemed hesitant to share some of her concerns with me, her adult and obviously hip and clued-in daughter. I gently reminded her that, after all, we were both grown women and that I only wanted her to enjoy life and all that being a woman had to offer, and that included sex. "Please," I said, "you can tell me anything."

And so she did. I guess I wasn't quite the hip and cool daughter I thought I was.

With that, I bid you good luck. Enjoy the conversation!

Questions

What do LesBiGays do in bed?

—⁓—

What turns you on in another man or woman?

—⁓—

If you're bi, does that mean you like sleeping
with men just as much as with women?
How are they different?

If you say you're attracted to women, why are you dating someone who looks so much like a man? Or vice versa?

—ɯ—

What was it like the first time you kissed another man/woman?

—ɯ—

What was it like when you first had sex with another man/woman?

—ɯ—

Do LesBiGays use sex toys a lot?

Are you worried about contracting or passing HIV or other sexually transmitted diseases? How do you deal with that risk?

—◊—

What's Lesbian Bed Death? Is it a myth or real?

—◊—

I've heard that LesBiGays are either "tops" or "bottoms"...what's that about, and what about you? And how do you know someone is a "top" or "bottom" before you sleep with them?

How can putting that *there* really feel good
to a guy?

—⊸⊸—

If you are attracted to both men and women,
does that mean you'll always be tempted
to mess around on your partner?

—⊸⊸—

Do you know anybody "on the down-low"?
How do they meet people to hook up
with if they're not out?

Honestly, don't you miss the "equipment" of the opposite sex? Is that why some people are bi?

"If you think you're missing anything, you can probably just mail-order it." – Angela

"Use your imagination...there's a lot we can do with the equipment we have." – Marcus

Afterword

That's it for QQST, but it's certainly not the end! I hope that these 108 questions are only the beginning of some wonderful conversations with your loved one. And perhaps you've already discovered that there are many, many more things to talk about.

I hope you'll share some of your Queer Questions – and straight talk – with me at www.QueerQuestionsStraightTalk.com.

Let's keep the conversation going.

Resources

There are many, many organizations out there working on behalf of LGBT and straight people, from local education and one-to-one counseling to national policy development. Here are just a few of the great nationally-based organizations who will be happy to hear from you.

GENERAL SUPPORT & INFORMATION

GLBT National Help Center: provides online chat and telephone support and peer counseling to LGBT and questioning people. Visit them at www.glnh.org or call their national hotline at (888) 843-4564. The Help Center also offers a youth hotline at (800) 246-PRIDE (7743).

The Trevor Project: promotes acceptance of LGBT and questioning youth and runs an accredited 24-hour crisis and suicide hotline. Visit them at www.thetrevorproject.org or call their Helpline at (866) 4-U-TREVOR (488-7386).

Trans Youth Family Allies: supports children, families and educators to develop environments where gender can be expressed and respected. Visit them at www.imatyfa.org.

Bisexual Resource Center: committed to providing support to the bisexual community and raising public awareness about bisexuality and bisexual people. The Bisexual Resource Center provides extensive information for and about bisexual people. Visit them at www.biresource.net or call at (617) 424-9595.

STUDENTS & SCHOOLS

Gay, Lesbian and Straight Education Network (GLSEN): focused on creating safe schools for all students. Visit them at www.glsen.org.

Gay-Straight Alliance Network (GSA Network): youth leadership organization that coordinates and helps students to build and sustain school-based gay-straight alliances. Visit them at www.gsanetwork.org.

Campus Pride: campus leadership organization that supports LGBT college and graduate students and their allies in creating more inclusive and LGBT-friendly universities. Visit them at www.campuspride.org.

FOR FAMILIES OF LGBT PEOPLE

Parents and Friends of Lesbians and Gays (PFLAG): promotes the health and wellbeing of gay, lesbian, bisexual and transgender persons, their families and friends through support, education and advocacy. Visit them at www.pflag.org or call (202) 467-8180.

COLAGE: a national movement of children, youth, and adults with one or more LGBT parents. COLAGE works toward social justice through youth empowerment, leadership development, education and advocacy. Visit them at www.colage.org.

LEGAL ADVOCACY & INFORMATION

Lambda Legal: a national organization committed to achieving full recognition of the civil rights of lesbians, gay men, bisexuals, transgender people and those with HIV, through impact litigation, education and public policy work. Visit them at www.lambdalegal.org or call their Help Desk at (866) 542-8336 (toll free).

National Center for Lesbian Rights (NCLR): a national legal organization committed to advancing the civil and human rights of lesbian, gay, bisexual, and transgender people and their families through litigation, public policy advocacy, and public education. Like Lambda Legal, NCLR provides legal information and referrals for Legal Helpline. Visit them at www.nclrights.org or call their legal helpline at (800) 528-6257.

Williams Institute at UCLA School of Law: a legal think tank dedicated to advancing sexual orientation law and public policy through rigorous, independent research and scholarship. An excellent resource for the most cutting edge information in LGBT research and policy. Visit them at www.law.ucla.edu/williamsinstitute.

PUBLIC POLICY, LEGISLATION & ACTIVISM

National Center for Transgender Equality (NCTE): dedicated to advancing the equality of transgender people through advocacy, collaboration and empowerment. NCTE supports transgender activism and education throughout the country as well as maintaining an activists' network. Visit them at www.transequality.org.

Human Rights Campaign (HRC): the largest LGBT rights organization in the country, focused on supporting pro-LGBT candidates and public policy. Visit them at www.hrc.org.

National Gay and Lesbian Task Force: builds grassroots power of LGBT community through trainings and by equipping state and local organizations with the skills they need to organize broad-based campaigns in support of LGBT legislation. Visit them at www.thetaskforce.org.

Gay and Lesbian Alliance Against Defamation (GLAAD): dedicated to promoting and ensuring fair, accurate and inclusive representation of people and events in the media as a means of eliminating homophobia and discrimination based on gender identity and sexual orientation.

Visit them at www.glaad.org.

HEALTH & HIV

The National Coalition for LGBT Health: provides a wide range of support, advocacy, policy development, research and education on the subject of LGBT health. Visit them at www.lgbthealth.net.

The Body – The Complete HIV/AIDS Resource: online database of a huge range of HIV resources, from dealing with the diagnosis, to cutting-edge research, to political action. Visit them at www.thebody.com.

Acknowledgments

This book is the product of thousands of conversations I've had with inquiring friends, family, colleagues and scoffers over the years. But to get all of that stuffed into the little book you are holding right now required the help, patience and wisdom of some particularly special people. I'd like to thank Karen Blum for knocking on all those virtual doors and being so very cheerful about it, Shannon Underberg and Mandy (you know who you are!) for writing beautifully about things I sometimes struggle to understand, Phoenix Schneider of the Trevor Project for showing me what the stakes really are for LGBT young people, and Rabbi Anson Laytner for his warm insights about family and love.

And for all their enthusiastic support and contributions, I'd like to give big hugs and thanks to: Michele Balan, Amanda Bearse, Laurie Bender, Dana Butler-Moburg, Marissa DeCuir, Carson Elder, Franco Giacomo Carbone, Angela Contreras, Margaret Hobart, Shari Herzfeld, Angie Horejsi, Kate Kendell, Carol Leifer, Paula McHale, Keith Owens, Anita Rellas, Elaine and Ed Samczyk, Julie Schoerke, Steve Silverman, Heidi Spurgin, Mary Sylla, Paul Tagliabue, Robbie Tarnove, Joey Watson, Holly Wensel, Marti Williams, Jeffrey Paul Wolff, and many others.

And finally, I want to give a special thank you to the three other people who conceived this book with me while sitting around eating cheesecake one September day in Pittsburgh: my publisher, Paul Kelly; my editor (and mom), Cathy Dees; and my partner, Traci Samczyk. Paul, you are a fab coach and a dear friend. Mom, the sex chapter notwithstanding, I hope we never ever stop tossing words and ideas back and forth. Traci, honey, you remind me every day what really counts.

About the Author

Abby Dees is a civil rights attorney and has been actively involved in lesbian, gay and bisexual rights and awareness work for 25 years. She has seen first hand that the best tools for understanding are courage, communication, patience and a good sense of humor – things that get drowned out too often by the loud squawk of politics.

Abby and her partner, Traci, are one of the 18,000 same-sex couples in California who married in 2008. Abby is a Beatles fanatic, failed rock star, and travels every chance she gets. She lives in Los Angeles and Nashville.